If you ask *The Little Book* a question it will answer you truthfully.

If you have a problem *The Little Book* will suggest a solution and show you the likely future outcome.

Although it has been used as an oracle for many thousands of years, *The Little Book* is much more than a guide to the future. It is a plan of The Universe, the wisest of wise counsellors and the truest of true friends.

No single mind can comprehend the I Ching nor presume to interpret it correctly. I therefore feel like the youthful torrent playing round the feet of the great Mountain of Hexagram 4 — and humbly apologize for the errors I have made.

RICHARD GILL

I·CHING

The Little Book
That Tells The Truth

RICHARD GILL

Aquarian/Thorsons
An Imprint of HarperCollins*Publishers*

I dedicate this work to King Wen
who, while cruelly imprisoned in the
year 1143 BC, first organized the
ancient images of the I Ching into a
book.

The Aquarian Press
An Imprint of HarperCollins*Publishers*
77—85 Fulham Palace Road,
Hammersmith, London W6 8JB

Published by The Aquarian Press 1993
3   5   7   9   10   8   6   4

© Richard Gill 1993
Illustrations © Anthony Clark 1993

Richard Gill asserts the moral right to
be identified as the author of this work

A catalogue record for this book
is available from the British Library

ISBN 1 85538 029 3 (pack)
ISBN 1 85538 030 7 (book)

Typeset by Harper Phototypesetters Limited
Northampton, England
Printed in Great Britain by
Woolnough Bookbinding Ltd,
Irthlingborough, Northamptonshire

Contents

The Illustrations

This book is illustrated with a series of I Ching paintings by Anthony Clark. These represent a visual interpretation of the meaning of each of the 64 Hexagrams, dispensing with the limitations of the written word in conveying a sense of meaning. Clearly a visual approach like this will be subject to the artist's own interpretation of the original, just like any new translation of the I Ching. But the paintings serve to embellish the meanings and offer an added dimension to one's use and enjoyment of the I Ching.

The full-colour cards from which the pictures have been taken do themselves make possible a simplified divination process. As you shuffle the pack, close your eyes and mentally ask your question. Then take a card from the deck, and study it to provide your answer. You can, of course, cross reference the card with the written meanings given in *The Little Book*. In particular, the Appendix on page 156 gives a succinct version of each card's advice, specifically created for use with the picture cards.

Although this is a very simplistic approach to the I Ching, it provides an alternative method of consultation, as valid as the yarrow stalks or the coins mentioned later, and the theory of meaningful correlation of events (page 20) holds good and will yield a correct answer.

Introduction

A Brief History of
The Little Book

The Little Book That Tells The Truth is the most modern work on a great discovery made 5,000 years ago in China.

Tradition gives the Emperor Fu Hsi (*c.* 3,000 BC) the credit for the initial invention. In reality, there must have been a concerted attempt by scholars of his period to explain the Universe and human life within it — and to express these findings in a succinct form. Eight visual images were devised to express the workings of Nature — DRAGON, EARTH, THUNDER, WATER, MOUNTAIN, WIND, FIRE and LAKE. To make these symbols manageable, a brilliant form of code was invented, based on the ancient polarity of Light and Darkness, Male and Female, Active and Passive, which the Chinese call *Yang* and *Yin*. Through a wonderful imaginative leap, which anticipated the invention of computer binary code by 5,000 years, Yang was expressed by a single unbroken line:

▬▬

. . . and Yin was expressed by a broken line:

▬ ▬

Just as a computer needs only the two symbols 0 and 1 to express any data fed into it, so the ancient Chinese found that they needed only the Yang and Yin lines to express their eight images:

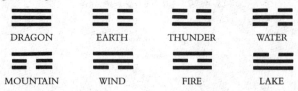

Manipulating these symbols, Fu Hsi discovered that the eight simple 'Trigrams' could be combined into 64 'Hexagrams', expressing 64 aspects of life and its changes. For example:

These images rapidly entered the national consciousness and were widely used for divination purposes. Their popularity probably accounts for the wide and beneficent influence of Yang and Yin on the early development of philosophy, medicine and art in China.

In 1143 BC, a remarkable Prince named Wen was cast into prison by the tyrant King Choe, last Emperor of the Shang Dynasty. In prison, Wen produced the first written version of the I Ching or 'Book of Life Changing'. He numbered and organized the 64 Hexagrams, gave them titles and, by long meditation on their inner significance, arrived at a verbal expression of their basic meaning. He was released from prison by his son Chou, who overthrew the Shang and, with his father's help, became the first Emperor of the great Chou Dynasty. The Chou ruled China for 800 years, a golden age of benevolent rule still fondly remembered today.

Chou's ability as a seer was no less remarkable than his

father's. Carrying on Wen's work, he arrived by intense meditation at a verbal expression of the six single lines which make up each Hexagram. Once expressed in words, the 'Book of Life Changing' made a tremendous impact on Chinese life. Its two great interpreters were, after all, Emperors ruling by its precepts — and during the Chou Dynasty, China was to produce both the moral teachings of Confucius and the tranquil insights of Taoism.

Indeed, the next great contributor to the Book was Confucius (541–479 BC). In old age, the Master declared that if he could live another 50 years, he would devote every moment to the study of the I Ching. In his experience, he said, the Book always told the truth — except perhaps on one occasion when it informed him that he was becoming a bore . . . ! Confucius added lengthy commentaries to the I Ching and is almost certainly the author of its 'Ten Wings', the erudite treatises that are now accepted as part of its traditional text.

In the academic world, however, earnest writings inspire more earnest writings — arguments, refutations, counter-refutations and *more* commentaries. In the careful Chinese way, all these were kept and incorporated into the text, so *The Little Book* became bigger and bigger. The more wordy and obscure it became, the more it delighted the street-corner fortune-tellers, who added complex rituals, diagrams, charts and arrangements of the Hexagrams to its lore.

Yet its basic strength held firm. Deeply religious yet completely secular, critical of authoritarianism yet supportive of authority, it proved great enough to survive wars, migrations, changing dynasties and a great burning of books in 213 BC. It has been in continual use in China for perhaps 5,000 years and still retains its place at the heart of Chinese culture.

In the 1920s it finally impinged on Western consciousness, thanks to a monumental translation by the German Richard Wilhelm. His 702 dense pages contain not only the traditional commentaries but Wilhelm's own comments upon them. This translation has deeply influenced all subsequent Western versions. C. Jung wrote an illuminating Foreword to Wilhelm's great work, and the I Ching became famous all over the world, a rich mine for psychologists and translators and scholarly Western commentators.

How far it has come from the simple visual code with which Fu Hsi could plot the workings of the Universe! Yet, despite the accretions of 3,000 years, the shining truth of those eight basic images remains unsullied. Despite the commentaries, the exquisite simplicity of Yang and Yin still tell their truthful story. These days we must dig deep to find it — but under all those words the crystal spring still bubbles joyfully.

This Version
of *The Little Book*

This book has been written because I use the I Ching daily and need a simple, clear and practical version, as truthful as possible in its response to the images. The following criteria have been used to put it together:

With the exception of the universally accepted Yin and Yang, I have eliminated all Chinese words. I find they add confusion, where all should be clear.

I have added no images and changed no imagery. I find the references to princes, officials, sages, palaces, thrones, chariots and horses perfectly intelligible to the modern mind. I deeply love the poetic images of Dragon, Earth, Thunder, Water, Mountain, Wind, Fire and Lake, finding them entirely satisfying. 'Sharpen your sword' will always remain a more immediate image than 'Load your machine-gun'.

However, where the I Ching uses the stuffy Confucian phrase 'The Superior Man', I have always paraphrased with

'You will be wise to . . .' or 'The wisest course will be . . .', which is implicit in the original. 'Concubines' *do* seem out of date and have been removed from my vocabulary.

I have used only the few brief words found necessary by Wen and Chou, their first great interpreters. The commentaries and treaties of Confucius and others are here in spirit but not in words. I find the *images* inspired and practical, the words mostly pedantic and obscure.

However, those words which Wen and Chou found it necessary to use have been painstakingly analysed, using six translations. Radical disagreements abound among the translators, for archaic Chinese is extremely cryptic. To incorporate different views and ensure that no relevant shade of meaning is lost, I have often found it necessary to use several English words to translate one in Chinese. I have also insisted that every sentence be grammatical and make sense (at least to me).

In counselling — a word I much prefer to 'divination' — doubt and ambiguity are enemies. I have sought to clarify the I Ching and I apologize most humbly if that has led me to make mistakes or appear dogmatic and over-confident. Please do not imagine that I regard this a 'correct' or 'finished' version: it is simply the clearest and most accurate that I can offer now.

Yang and Yin

The Little Book's picture of the Universe is
briefly as follows:

All is One. Everything is an apparent part of One
Reality. As One cannot see itself, it manifests eternally,
becoming apparently two — Subject to perceive;
Object to be perceived. From this Source, the eternal
manifestation of duality, springs all creation.

The One is Absolute Stillness but creation is in
constant change. The One can be represented by this
symbol:

The two halves of this Whole are called Yang
and Yin.

They are opposite yet complementary.

Yang is Creative, Masculine, Active, and Light.

Yin is Receptive, Feminine, Passive and Dark.

Yang is represented by the single line ━━━ .

Yin is represented by the broken line ━ ━ .

Yang and Yin together make up the whole
Universe, which is in constant change due to the
fluctuations of Yang and Yin. Any object, person,
event, situation, thought or emotion is a mixture of
Yang and Yin qualities.

The Images of Nature

The Trigrams

The principal powers of nature are all combinations of Yang and Yin. There are eight such powers, so their Yang—Yin balance is expressed in eight three-line combinations called 'Trigrams'.

Dragon

THE DRAGON is entirely Yang and represents *creative action*. He is the noble power of light and air, imagination and will, entirely masculine. In Chinese mythology, he controls the clouds and waters and is, if not benign, certainly not malevolent like the European dragon. As the Creative Principle he is the Father of all things.

Earth

EARTH is entirely Yin and represents *fertility*. She is dark and devoted, warm and receptive. She is the Mother of all things.

Fortune-tellers ascribe endless subsidiary meanings to these powerful images. MOUNTAIN, for example, represents 'Hand' or 'Dog' or 'The colour Purple'. I find no basis for these additions in the original text. However, if DRAGON and EARTH are the Father and Mother of all things, then perhaps the Yang-dominated Trigrams can be seen as their sons and perhaps the Yin-dominated Trigrams can be seen as their daughters.

In any Trigram the *single* line is dominant, controlling the two weaker lines. Thus the Trigrams with one Yang line against two Yin lines are Yang or male — the sons. And the Trigrams with only one Yin line are female — the daughters.

Trigrams are always constructed and read from the bottom up. So the first son will be THUNDER, whose dominant line falls in the first or bottom line.

Thunder

THUNDER, the eldest son, represents *turbulence*, shock and arousement.

Water or Chasm

WATER or CHASM, the middle son, represents *danger* or a deep, dark pit.

Mountain

MOUNTAIN the youngest son, represents *stillness*. This

quality has both positive and negative aspects, representing the highest peak of spiritual attainment versus an obstinate refusal to move.

Wind or Wood

WIND or WOOD, the eldest daughter, represents *gentleness*. This quality has positive and negative aspects representing persistent endeavour versus timidity and indecision.

Fire

FIRE, the middle daughter, represents *warmth*, clarity and affection.

Lake

LAKE, the youngest daughter, represents *joy*, purity and truth.

The powers represented by these eight basic images make up the natural Universe.

Note that WATER is also CHASM and that WIND is also WOOD. It is almost as though positive and negative aspects of these images were expressed in their very names. WATER is a positive force for good in the oceans and in rain, while CHASM is a negative force, deep and dangerous. WIND is intangible and restless and therefore negative, while WOOD represents the natural growth of trees and the positive craftsmanship of the carpenter.

The Hexagrams

The eight Trigrams, the symbolic essence of the I Ching, can be placed one above another to form 64 different six-line combinations called 'Hexagrams'.

Each of the Hexagrams has a title, an image and a basic meaning. A complete index of the Hexagrams will be found on page 160, but here are two examples:

Hexagram 11 – EARTH over DRAGON

Title: *HARMONY*

Subsidiary Titles: Prosperity. Safety. Peace.

Image: The Dragon sleeps, deep underground. His protection gives warmth and safety to all.

Basic Meaning: The small and mean now end and the great and good now come, bringing peaceful progress, success and prosperity.

Study this carefully. The image is important because it tells you *why* the basic symbols of EARTH and DRAGON in this relationship produce *harmony*. The basic meaning is a verbal expression of the influence of *harmony*. on a particular time or situation.

Now look at the opposing Hexagram:

Hexagram 12 – DRAGON over EARTH

Title: *STAGNATION*

Subsidiary Titles: Obstruction. Stand-off. Implacable opposition.

Image: Small, mean and unwelcoming, the earthlings drive off the flying dragon.

Basic Meaning: Evil people are blocking your way. Be steadfast in retreat, for the great and good now end and the small and mean now come.

The two great forces, so harmoniously placed in Hexagram 11, here send each other flying apart, like magnets repelling each other. Note also how EARTH is reflected into 'The men of earth' or 'earthlings', a typical example of the way in which the basic images can be transformed into aspects of themselves.

If these beautiful symbols seem alien at first, please persevere. To me they quickly became a natural language, modern and universal.

Images Within Images: The Individual Lines

Each Hexagram is made up of six individual lines. These lines, when *The Little Book* draws special attention to them, are of utmost importance. They each have an image, usually deriving directly from the basic image of their Hexagram. Once again, it is these images that carry the meaning.

Hexagram 48 – Thirst at the Well

In Hexagram 48 all six individual lines refer directly to a well. It is muddy and undrinkable in the bottom line, full to the top and good to drink in the sixth line.

In other Hexagrams it may seem that the images of the individual lines bear no relation to the basic image. In fact, this is never so. For example, pigs, fishes, guests, flaying, melons, sun, shade and horns all figure in the imagery of the individual lines of Hexagram 44:

Hexagram 44 – Being Carried Away

This Hexagram has confounded commentators across the centuries. In my translation I have tried to show *how* each image relates to 'being carried away' and to its linear place in the Hexagram. The development of these images, once perceived, is perfectly logical.

If you read other translations of Hexagram 44 you will see how an insistence on translating Chou's *word* has sometimes led to a rejection of the *image* he indicates. I stress again: the I Ching is not verbal. Words are mental tools, limited and limiting, while a symbol can contain a Universe and provide a focus for a lifetime's contemplation. Words are needed to indicate what treasure lies within an image, but the fewer words used, the better. That is why Wen and Chou wrote a *Little Book*. I have followed their example.

The Little Book
That Tells The Truth

Over the millennia a rich tradition of ritual and ceremony
has grown up around the I Ching:

Preliminary rituals and ceremonies

Richard Wilhelm and John Blofeld both give descriptions
in their books (see the Bibliography, p.159). I find them
fascinating. However, the I Ching is concerned with truth
and I am unable to truthfully perform these ancient rites.

Consultation by division of 50 yarrow stalks

John Blofeld's book contains an admirable description of
this ancient process, should you wish to adopt it.

Consultation by tossing three coins

Most books contain descriptions of this method, should
you wish to adopt it.

Traditional way of writing the hexagrams and moving lines

Wilhelm and Blofeld both describe this in their books.

I found 6 and 9, X and O extremely clumsy when I began work on the I Ching, and still do.

Unable to find any justification for these methods in the original text — and finding them confusing where all should be most clear — I see no purpose in perpetuating them here. All that *The Little Book* requires is a clear method of constructing the original Hexagram and of determining the Moving Lines.

However, I feel bound to make it clear that most serious students of the I Ching would gravely disapprove of the simpler method that I have developed in this book. I can only say that it has been continually approved by the I Ching itself and that it works most effectively.

How *The Little Book* Looks into the Future

I accept the basis of Taoist philosophy! To my modern mind — and to quantum physics — it seems self-evident that the Universe is One. There *must* be One Reality, containing an infinite multiplicity of appearances . . .

If this is so, then *anything* occurring *anywhere* must in essence be one with all other apparent happenings, past, present and future. And if this is so, the tiniest event — physical, mental or spiritual — must register the effect of every past happening and will itself affect every future happening. 'Coincidence' and 'accident' then cease to exist, for every tiny event becomes meaningful.

If you accept this premise, as I do, it follows that a certain card turned over by a certain hand, at a certain time, in response to a certain question is a meaningful effect of the Universe in action. And if that card has been specially created to carry information recording where it came from and where it is going to, then it will both record and interpret that meaning for us. With such an instrument we can trace past causes and predict future effects.

That is exactly what *The Little Book* is — eight images bearing coded information about their own causes and effects. These eight images create 64 Hexagrams, each of which can stay as it is or change into any one of the other 63. So there are 4,096 possible set 'answers' to an infinite number of 'questions', each of which colours the set answer with its unique specifics . . .

To use a modern metaphor, the images and Hexagrams are both the computer *and* its non-verbal data and the 64 texts are the verbal print-out. As that print-out is 'set', little room is left for erroneous interpretation of the data, to which other forms of divination are so prone.

In my belief, that is why *The Little Book* is so valuable; that is how it works; and that is why it tells the truth.

Asking Your Question

Before you do anything else, write down the question you wish to ask. Make sure that it contains no ambiguities or double questions. Make it as specific as possible, mentioning dates, names and places — but keep it short. Avoid questions requiring a 'Yes or No' answer. The most fruitful questions tend to start 'Should I do such-and-such?' or 'What will happen if . . .?' or 'What is the likely outcome of such-and-such a plan?'

If you prefer, you may ask no question at all. *The Little Book* will automatically respond to the major issue of your life and advise on your general situation.

Obtaining Your Answer

1. Take the eight IMAGE CARDS with the Trigrams from the deck. The dominant line in each Trigram is given under its name. It is this dominant line that principally concerns you when using the Cards. Note that it is

always the *single* line that dominates and indicates whether the Trigram is basically Yin or Yang. Dragon is obviously Yang, of course, and Earth is obviously Yin.

2. Mix the cards face-down on a tray or tablecloth — or simply in your hand. As you mix them, mentally ask your question. If you feel drawn to any particular card, turn it up. If not, pick a card at random and turn it up. I usually shut my eyes or look away while making a choice.

3. You have turned one image face up. If the dominant line is Yang, draw an unbroken Yang line onto your paper (remembering that it will be the *bottom* line and that five further lines must be added on top of it):

▬▬▬▬

If the dominant line is Yin, draw a broken line onto the paper:

▬▬ ▬▬

If the Image is DRAGON, draw a Yang line and mark its significance with a dot on your own paper:

▬▬▬▬ •

If the Image is EARTH, draw a Yin line and mark its significance with a dot on your paper:

▬▬ ▬▬ •

The dotted DRAGON and EARTH lines have great significance. These are the lines that are in dynamic movement, thereby changing the present into the future. For this reason they are called 'Moving Lines'.

4. Replace the card, reshuffle, then repeat the entire process five times until you have written six lines and therefore created a complete Hexagram. This encapsulates, in code, the answer to your question. So you can put the image cards away.

5. If you have marked no Moving Lines there is nothing further to do at this stage: your coded answer is complete. But if any Moving Lines occur — and you may have none, or one, or two, three, four, five or six — then draw a *second* Hexagram in which all the Moving Lines (the ones with your dots beside them) transform into their opposite. So a dotted Yang line becomes a Yin line in the second Hexagram and a dotted Yin line becomes a Yang line in the second Hexagram, creating an entirely new Hexagram. For example:

First Hexagram   *Second Hexagram*

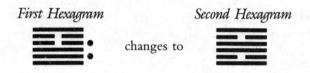

changes to

You now have your complete answer, in coded form. All that remains is to translate it.

Translating Your Answer

1. Check the chart at the back of the book. If EARTH forms the Upper Trigram in the first Hexagram and MOUNTAIN the Lower Trigram, the chart asks you to refer to Hexagram 15 in *The Little Book*.
2. I strongly advise you to write down and date your answer, for future reference. First, write down the Hexagram title, paying full attention to its subsidiary meanings. Then, if no Moving Lines have occurred, simply write down the basic meaning of your Hexagram — and your answer is complete.
3. However, if any Moving Lines *did* occur, ignore the basic meaning and write down the full text of *each*

indicated Moving Line, starting with the lowest.

4. As the Moving Lines created an entirely new, second Hexagram, look this up in the chart, too.

    Write down the second Hexagram title and its basic meaning. This completes the verbal expression of your answer.

The Interpretation

Your answer can be interpreted as follows:

"At a present time of — TITLE OF YOUR FIRST HEXAGRAM — you are especially advised that — *the text of the Moving Lines* (or, if no Moving Lines are given, *the basic meaning* which, in this case only, will complete your answer).

"The likelihood is that the situation is changing to a time of — TITLE OF THE SECOND HEXAGRAM — in which the probable result and appropriate course of action will be — *the basic meaning of the second Hexagram.*"

The situation can also be expressed by THE FIRST IMAGE developing into THE SECOND IMAGE. The images are, of course, poetic, yet they express the full depth of the I Ching's insight in a uniquely pure and direct form. They can sometimes be more illuminating than the practical advice derived from them and I urge you to study and explore them.

Using the Answer

The Little Book can give detailed answers of extraordinary relevance, but its purpose is not to amaze you but to help and advise. One of its most important qualities is that it can make you think in new directions: I have often found that as one studies an answer, helpful new ideas come into one's mind.

A concentrated, conscious study of the answer somehow releases the inner meaning of the images, both to the subconscious and *from* the subconscious. Properly used, *The Little Book* induces a state of meditative contemplation which is itself extremely valuable. If each word and image is deeply absorbed, rather as one absorbs a poem, then calm and confidence are generated. These form the best possible basis for insight, clear judgement and correct action.

Some Problems of Interpretation

1. In *The Little Book* pronouns and gender are interchangeable. 'He' can mean 'she', 'we' or 'you', and vice versa.

   Similarly, the tenses of the verbs are not to be taken literally. For example, 'He did this' often means 'He *does* this' or 'He *will* do this.' As an answer moves from the present into the future, it is usually clear which tense is intended. A good clear question usually prevents problems of gender and time occurring.

2. Always write down the answer *exactly* as given: do not be tempted to alter genders and tenses as you write. The great virtue of *The Little Book* is that it eliminates wishful thinking and inaccurate subjective interpretations. You can add a mental interpretation later, but it is best to record the words exactly as they occur.

3. Sometimes an answer may seem quite inappropriately severe or euphoric, or totally irrelevant, or quite incomprehensible. When this happens, the I Ching may have picked up a major problem in your life and may have chosen to comment on this instead of on the minor question you have asked. It may also be answering a question you have subconsciously repressed because it is dangerous or unpleasant. Or it may be announcing an 'out-of-the-blue event' that your conscious mind

can know nothing of and therefore cannot interpret.

Such answers are rare — but they should be studied with particular care. If, after long study, your conscious mind cannot perceive any meaning that has relevance, I advise you to ignore this answer completely and, above all, *not to worry about it.* Keep what you have written down and study it again in a few weeks — or a few months — or a few years. In the end, light will dawn and you will agree with Confucius that *The Little Book* always tells the truth.

Further Advice

1. Most experts approach the I Ching in a ritualistic way. This is not necessary. However, I recommend that the image cards be kept carefully or wrapped in a clean cloth when not in use; that your hands are always clean when using them; and that you do not let other people handle your image cards. I have always preferred to mix and turn the cards myself, while the questioner mentally asks his question, but there are no 'rules' that need be obeyed. All that matters is that you are true to yourself in your choice of procedures: then you will automatically be true to the I Ching.

2. Ask questions only about matters of significance. Never ask questions for fun.

3. Never repeat a question to *The Little Book*. If an answer seems obscure, rephrase it and ask it again the next day.

4. A curious phenomenon: although *The Little Book* induces a feeling of beneficent relaxation, consulting it is actually *extremely hard work*. It literally takes something out of you, though I am at a loss to say what that something is. If you question it for too long, the sensation of being spiritually drained is uniquely unpleasant. Please limit yourself to a maximum of three questions a day — and never ask a question when tired.

The Little Book That
Tells The Truth

Creative Action

CREATIVE JOY. PRODUCTIVE PLANNING.
FATHERHOOD.

 DRAGON over DRAGON suggests: Two dragons playing: light, fire and joy.

BASIC MEANING

To persevere in this righteous and creative course will lead to supreme success.

MOVING LINES

Sixth: A reckless dragon. Too much energy has been released too fast. You will regret it if you do not moderate this reckless display of strength.

↑ **Fifth:** A dragon in flight across the sky. Your project is under way, blessed and successful: nevertheless, you will be wise to discuss its progress with an expert.

↑ **Fourth:** A dragon crouching to leap — but which way will he choose? Up into the sky or down into the earth? Both are in his power and either will be a correct choice. He alone can decide.

↑ **Third:** A wakeful dragon. There is danger — not least from your own over-ambitious ideas and complacency. However, it can be averted if you are intensely active all day long and remain alert throughout the night.

↑ **Second:** A dragon stirring. When great ideas start to stir, it will be wise to seek advice from an expert.

↑ **Bottom:** A dragon hiding. Do not reveal your great ideas yet. Do not act yet.

·2·

Fertility

RECEPTIVITY. GROWTH IN THE DARK. MOTHERHOOD.
DEVOTED SERVICE.

 EARTH over EARTH suggests: The depths of the earth — dark, silent and warm.

30

BASIC MEANING

To be devoted yet strong, like a young mother, brings supreme success. If you try to take the initiative you will go astray, but if you gladly follow you will find true guidance. Peaceful devotion and quiet, enduring strength bring great good fortune.

MOVING LINES

Sixth Dragons should be the devoted servants of heaven. When they fight, their blood — the black and the yellow — creates a wilderness on earth. Neither can defeat the other — and everyone suffers.

↑ **Fifth** Absolute discretion and trustworthiness bring great good fortune.

↑ **Fourth** Seek no praise and earn no blame. Give no praise and lay no blame. Just tie up this sack: if you take great care, its contents will not harm you.

↑ **Third** Hide your worth: finish the work but claim no credit.

↑ **Second** Let nature work: though she does nothing, all her affairs prosper.

↑ **Bottom** When the grass is frosty underfoot, the first ice is not far away: prepare for winter now.

A Difficult Beginning

BIRTH PAINS. ADVERSE CONDITIONS.
CONFUSION AT THE START.

 WATER over THUNDER suggests:
Tempests above and earthquakes below —
cruel conditions for seeds and saplings.

BASIC MEANING

This troubled start will lead to great success and prosperity in the end, if you do not change direction or start anything new. Persist untiringly in your present righteous course – but recognize that you need help and that the situation should be consolidated.

MOVING LINES

Sixth Your horse breaks out of the wagon and deserts. Weeping tears of blood, you abandon the journey. This is truly sad – but the best thing is to make a clean break and start again.

↑ **Fifth** You have scared support away with these traveller's tales and grandiose promises. If you plan modest journeys – good fortune; if you persist in over-ambitious plans – misfortune.

↑ **Fourth** Ride out and look for a wagon and a wife – you need them if you would grasp this splendid opportunity. With their help you will win good fortune on this journey: everything is entirely favourable.

↑ **Third** Hunting deer without a guide, you lose your way in the forest. It is wise to go no further – for you will meet with failure if you persist in the hunt.

↑ **Second** Mounting difficulties: your horse bucks, jolting and jarring you, taking you and your wagon round in circles. Don't be frightened of one who comes running to help you – he is not a robber! – but don't fall into his arms and agree to marry him, either. For success on this journey you will need to stay chaste for ten years or more.

↑ **Bottom** You are right to hesitate: this is the right road but you should not attempt to travel it alone. Offer your help to other travellers and make the journey together, for mutual support and safety.

·4·

Inexperience

CHILDISHNESS. IGNORANCE. FOLLY.

 MOUNTAIN over WATER suggests: The mountain smiles quietly down at the water rushing round its feet.

BASIC MEANING

Youth – or inexperience – achieves progress and success, especially if the tyro is prepared to seek guidance, not to question his teacher's advice, nor ask too many questions. The teacher, for his part, should gladly give guidance – though only if approached – ensure that he is making himself clear and encourage the student to stand on his own feet as soon as possible.

MOVING LINES

Sixth It is important that further transgressions be prevented — but don't be too harsh: it would be wrong and dangerous to punish unjustly or in anger or revenge.

↑ **Fifth** Innocent folly leads to good fortune. So does a humble and obedient approach to the wise.

↑ **Fourth** It will be wise to offer no further advice: the obstinate youngster must be left to learn his lesson the hard way.

↑ **Third** You should not marry a girl who flings herself at you; she may be impressed principally by your wealth or status. Nor should you behave in this way: there is no lasting value in such affections.

↑ **Second** Good fortune comes from handling the inexperienced very gently. However, they should be given scope: this youngster is quite capable of taking charge of the houschold. Taking a young wife is blessed.

↑ **Bottom** A youngster needs firm discipline — even punishment. But the shackles should not stay on for long, or damage will be done.

· 5 ·

Waiting

PATIENCE. CONSERVING ENERGY. CALCULATED INACTION.

 WATER over DRAGON suggests: The dragon sleeps while waiting for the storm to break.

BASIC MEANING

Resolute patience, conservation of energy and avoidance of all precipitate action will bring brilliant success and good fortune in the end. Wait calmly for time to reveal what it is you must do – then a major move or decisive action will prove advantageous.

MOVING LINES

Sixth Unable to wait, you enter the darkness. Be prepared for three unexpected occurrences — strangers or strange events — for, if you are alert to their possibilities, they can save you.

↑ **Fifth** Waiting at the feast. You will gain in strength and determination if, while waiting for the onslaught, you can eat, drink and make merry. Good fortune comes from such wise use of time — but, of course, you must not relax your vigilance.

↑ **Fourth** Waiting in blood. The only way to survive this onslaught is to defend yourself stoically, waiting for the enemy to withdraw.

↑ **Third** Waiting in the mud. Take care: to dig trenches and keep guards in them may deplete your strength and invite an enemy attack.

↑ **Second** Waiting on the sands. When enemy movements are detected across the river, it is wise to keep lookouts posted along its bank. There may be some criticism but such precautions will bring good fortune in the end.

↑ **Bottom** Waiting in the fields. The danger is still far away. Let normal work continue in the village fields, for all unusual action should be avoided.

·6·

Conflict

DISAGREEMENT. A QUARREL. LITIGATION.

 DRAGON over WATER suggests: A chasm challenges the flying dragon: let him beware, for it is dangerous.

BASIC MEANING

You know yourself to be right but face obstruction and opposition. Good fortune comes only through extreme apprehension and caution so, if humanly possible, stop, calm down and compromise – for if you take this conflict through to the end you will meet with disaster. A wise arbiter will help but no move or major action can bring you any advantage.

MOVING LINES

Sixth: Maybe you triumph: maybe you are rewarded: but such a victory is hollow. It does you little credit and brings no happiness — for this feud will be renewed again and again and again.

↑ **Fifth** Seek a just arbiter: this conflict will bring you great good fortune.

↑ **Fourth** Don't torment yourself by struggling on: even if you win, you won't be happy. Remember your ideals: peace — and therefore good fortune — will be found in ceasing to struggle and in a calm acceptance that you cannot change your fate.

↑ **Third** Don't compete for promotion: just rely on good, old-fashioned obedience and selfless service. There may be problems now but good fortune will be yours in the end.

↑ **Second** You are unequal to this struggle. You will make no mistake — and will save family, friends and colleagues much trouble — if you back down and simply return home.

↑ **Bottom** Say as little as possible and don't let this develop into a quarrel. You may suffer some small dent in your pride or reputation — but in the end good fortune comes from declining this argument.

Arming Your Forces

A Need For Discipline. Preventing a Collapse.

 EARTH over WATER suggests: A village over a subterranean chasm: danger of collapse.

BASIC MEANING

To win good fortune you must have steadfast discipline and a strong, experienced leader. When both are present no mistakes will be made.

MOVING LINES

Sixth A wise general will promote only those who support him. Opponents or critics should not be given posts of command, even in peacetime.

↑ **Fifth** Bandits are spying out your fields: the wisest course is to ride out and seize them. A veteran should lead. If younger men hang back or operate wildly, refusing to join an organized force, disaster will follow.

↑ **Fourth** The army is correct to make a strategic retreat.

↑ **Third** This army has too many leaders. Such a dead-weight of incompetence leads to disaster.

↑ **Second** This is his third command – and the leader is where he should be, in the middle of his forces. Such behaviour creates confidence and good fortune.

↑ **Bottom** An army sets out. If it is sufficiently disciplined – success; if it is not – disaster.

· 8 ·

Mutual Help

NEIGHBOURLINESS. A SENSE OF COMMUNITY.
UNITED ACTION.

 WATER over EARTH suggests: Men on earth should combine to ward off the tempest.

42

BASIC MEANING

When trouble threatens, safety and good fortune can be found by grouping together. Therefore join, form or strengthen a group now: if you leave it too late you will deeply regret it. If necessary, question the I Ching again to discover whether you yourself have the drive, strength and integrity to lead such a group.

MOVING LINES

Sixth Fatal hesitation: if no-one is willing to form a group and hold it together, the chance to unite is lost and serious misfortune follows.

↑ **Fifth** This is a fine group, united around a fine leader. Don't pursue those who do not wish to join: you have no need of them. Good fortune will be gained.

↑ **Fourth** Keep striving to bring outsiders into this group: their extra strength will bring good fortune.

↑ **Third** The group you belong to is of very questionable worth.

↑ **Second** Work hard to keep this group together: it is worth it. Good fortune comes from continuing this valuable work.

↑ **Bottom** You will make no mistake to be loyal to this group: like you, its members are full of sincerity and good intentions. Unexpected good fortune comes from this association.

·9·

Mild Restraint

IRKSOME RESTRICTIONS.
A WEAKNESS THAT HINDERS PROGRESS.
VERSUS – A CALMING INFLUENCE.

 WIND over DRAGON suggests: Stroking his back, the wind lulls the mighty dragon to sleep.

44

BASIC MEANING

A gentle approach brings progress and success in the end. The breeze wafts dense clouds in from the west – but the blessed rain does not fall yet.

MOVING LINES

Sixth The rains seemed gentle – but now the roads are impassable. However virtuous your cause, however necessary your journey, rest now. If you persist in advancing you will get bogged down and disaster will follow (especially if you are female and especially in the next four weeks).

↑ **Fifth** Your openness and generosity attract others to your cause. You are enriched by this support and will be able to help others.

↑ **Fourth** Openness and honesty avert a dangerous quarrel and banish all anxieties.

↑ **Third** The spokes of your wheels were too weak: they break and fall out. At this enforced halt there is discord between man and wife.

↑ **Second** Let yourself be led back to the true path: it leads to good fortune.

↑ **Bottom** You won't be blamed if you quietly return to your own, original path: it leads to good fortune.

10

Treading Carefully

TAKING A RISK.

 DRAGON over LAKE suggests: The flying dragon risks a ducking, skimming so low across the lake.

BASIC MEANING

If you take great care you can tread on the tail of this tiger and live to enjoy success.

MOVING LINES

Sixth Review the lessons of the journey behind you — and study the way ahead before you move on. When you are certain that the way is clear, advance: it will lead to supreme good fortune.

↑ **Fifth** You are on the right path — but be aware that it is dangerous. Confidence and resolution are essential.

↑ **Fourth** With extreme care and caution you can tread on the tail of this tiger and survive to win good fortune.

↑ **Third** Having only one eye, you believe you see properly: having one lame leg, you believe you can run. But you neither see this tiger, nor can escape him. If you tread on his tail you will be terribly bitten. Take care that a superior, or a strongly held ideal, does not send you into danger.

↑ **Second** If you want a peaceful life and good fortune, stick to the straight and level path.

↑ **Bottom** To go forward simply, sticking to your accustomed path, is the best way to progress, for such behaviour invites no criticism.

11

Harmony

PROSPERITY. SAFETY. PEACE.

 EARTH over DRAGON suggests: The dragon sleeps, deep underground. His protection gives warmth and safety to all.

BASIC MEANING

The small and mean now end and the great and good now come, bringing peaceful progress, success and prosperity.

MOVING LINES

Sixth The defences of your village are crumbling. Don't attempt to fight off the bandits — strive only to maintain order and to repair the damage. You may blame yourself and be blamed by others — but an uncomfortable peace is far better than the ruin you will suffer if you continue to fight.

↑ **Fifth** When a princess gladly marries a commoner and obeys him with delight, peace, prosperity and supreme good fortune come to the realm.

↑ **Fourth** You may have to live among neighbours far less prosperous than you have been. Seize this chance gladly and with humility, taking care not to demonstrate any superiority over them. Harmony among neighbours is essential — you may need each other's help at any time.

↑ **Third** Every hill has its downward slope and prosperity, too, may dwindle or change. Do not let this disturb your inner peace: enjoy the good fortune you still possess.

↑ **Second** Be patient and magnanimous if attacked by uncultivated people — yet ford the river resolutely, without boats if need be. Turn your thoughts to the future and to distant places — yet remember your comrades and be completely fair and considerate towards them. This is the middle way and for the sake of preserving peace you are advised to take it.

↑ **Bottom** Grass cannot truly be uprooted for the earth in which it grows comes up with the roots, ready for re-planting. Do not fear that peace and prosperity will be lost if you make a major move: they will accompany you — and such a new venture will bring good fortune.

·12·

Stagnation

Obstruction. Stand-off. Implacable Opposition.

 DRAGON over EARTH suggests: Small, mean and unwelcoming, the earthlings drive off the flying dragon.

BASIC MEANING

Evil people are blocking your way. Be steadfast in retreat – for the great and good now end and the small and mean now come.

MOVING LINES

Sixth Your efforts successfully end the standstill: joy and good fortune.

↑ **Fifth** The standstill is ending. You can take advantage of this change, but be aware that you will need to plant many seedlings and stake them most securely if one is to survive. If you take such precautions – good fortune and success.

↑ **Fourth** If you follow this wise suggestion and act to put an end to the standstill, you will greatly help yourself and others.

↑ **Third** If you can endure this shame, things will improve.

↑ **Second** Inferior people will do anything, however shameful, to curry favour. If you can bear this setback patiently, you will win success in the end.

↑ **Bottom** You are uprooted but, as with a clump of grass, the rich earth you have grown in will come away with you. With steadfastness and loyalty, good fortune and success will come of this.

·13·

Welcome

COMRADESHIP. ALLIANCE. LOVE. UNION.

 DRAGON over FIRE suggests: A fire lit below to welcome the flying dragon.

BASIC MEANING

Open affection and open discussion bring comradeship and success. A move or new association is favoured. Remain open, honest and honourable always.

MOVING LINES

Sixth Welcoming these people to a walk in the meadows is safer than inviting them home.

↑ **Fifth** The alliance starts with open disagreement and tears — but it will end in laughter. After great struggles, you succeed in collaborating and win a victory.

↑ **Fourth** You can hardly take an army with you to meet this person — but you will be wise to welcome him from the top of stout walls: good fortune comes of such caution.

↑ **Third** To keep weapons concealed and to welcome people from the top of a high hill shows apparent openness but actual mistrust. It leads to three years in which no progress can be made.

↑ **Second** If you are welcomed into a clique, or allow a clique to form, you will bitterly regret it.

↑ **Bottom** Welcome new friends at your gate: there can be no harm in such free and open gatherings.

·14·

Great Possessions

 FIRE over DRAGON suggests: The dragon's radiance lights up the sky.

BASIC MEANING

To him who is blessed, great blessings come: prosperity and supreme success.

MOVING LINES

Sixth You are greatly blessed: good fortune and success in everything.

↑ **Fifth** It is sincerity — not wealth and show — that attracts and inspires others. Behave with dignity and good fortune will result.

↑ **Fourth** Don't try to keep up with those who are better off than you — and be tactful and modest when among people who have less.

↑ **Third** Use your treasure for the good of all: don't hold onto things that other people may need more — it would be shameful.

↑ **Second** Now you have got large carts and many helpers you will make no mistake to load up and set off.

↑ **Bottom** New wealth and position come to you. Take real care to recognize the dangers and responsibilities they bring — and do not become arrogant or wasteful.

Modesty

MODERATION. SEEKING A JUST BALANCE.

 EARTH over MOUNTAIN suggests: Earth carried from a mountain-top raises the plain and lowers the mountain.

BASIC MEANING

Modesty brings success. The great and the humble should both act with moderation if they would bring their affairs to a satisfactory conclusion.

MOVING LINES

Sixth What use is a cock too modest to crow loudly? Don't be too meek: energetic action is needed if you are to keep control of your realm.

↑ **Fifth** Be generous — but not showy; punish — but do not be severe. If you punish moderately and reward moderately, everything is entirely favourable.

↑ **Fourth** True moderation reveals itself in cautious, modest action — not in a refusal to act. If you take such action now, everything is entirely favourable.

↑ **Third** Hard work and a low profile are needed to bring this affair to a satisfactory conclusion: good fortune.

↑ **Second** What use is a cock too modest to crow loudly? Don't be too meek: a firm stand will lead to good fortune.

↑ **Bottom** If you act with extreme humility a major move will not be impeded and will lead to good fortune.

·16·

Enthusiasm

PROFOUND AND LASTING ENTHUSIASM.
VERSUS - A PASSING WHIM. AN ENJOYABLE EXCURSION.
A LACK OF REAL ENTHUSIASM.

 THUNDER over EARTH suggests: Music thunders across the plain: a day of festival and joyous relaxation.

BASIC MEANING

To make this plan succeed you need helpers – and must be so truly enthusiastic that you can enthuse others.

MOVING LINES

Sixth Your enthusiasm is misplaced. Luckily, you wake up before it is too late.

↑ **Fifth** Deficient enthusiasm – still you persist. Frustrated enthusiasm – still you don't die.

↑ **Fourth** This plan could enthuse everyone and bring you the greatest satisfaction: friends would gather round you and you could achieve great things.

↑ **Third** Real enthusiasm expresses itself in action, not in vague hopes or dependence on others. You will regret it if you day-dream or hesitate now.

↑ **Second** Real enthusiasm is as solid as a rock. Be prudent, of course, but stand firm on your beliefs: good fortune will result before the end of the day.

↑ **Bottom** Boasting brings misfortune.

17

Following

FOLLOWING A LEAD. LEADING A FOLLOWING.
ACTING AS CIRCUMSTANCES DICTATE.

 LAKE over THUNDER suggests: Thunder under the lake — ripple after ripple after ripple.

BASIC MEANING

Whether you lead or whether you follow, let yourself be led now, for following brings supreme success. However, do not be led astray: you must take only that path you know to be right and follow it to the end.

MOVING LINES

Sixth The king humbles himself and follows the sage to the holy mountain. The sage, so honoured, is bound to follow the king back when he returns. Such honourable following should bring joy to the realm — but in practice it seems to dissipate spiritual power and to sap the energy of the ruler.

↑ **Fifth** You follow a blessed path: good fortune.

↑ **Fourth** You follow or are followed for wrong, selfish reasons. To persevere with such a following will lead to misfortune. There can be nothing wrong in taking a clear look at the situation and in acting honestly to end it.

↑ **Third** You will find what you seek if you follow the strong and resolutely leave the weak behind. Let your children go and cling to your husband.

↑ **Second** Following the weak, you lose the strong. Clinging to your child, you lose your husband.

↑ **Bottom** A new leader appears or a new path opens. To follow it with determination brings good fortune, especially if it encourages you to step outside your own front door to associate with other people.

18

Repairing the Damage

RESTORING ONESELF. SCOURING AWAY CORRUPTION.
A NEW BROOM SWEEPING CLEAN.

 MOUNTAIN over WIND suggests: Wind
scouring out a mountain valley.

BASIC MEANING

Supreme success will result if you take bold action to remove or repair the damage caused by previous mistakes. A major move or journey is greatly favoured. Three days' hard thought before and three days' hard work after are needed to ensure that what went wrong before does not happen again.

MOVING LINES

Sixth If you wish to preserve your integrity do not serve kings or princes.

↑ **Fifth** A son striving to deal with inherited problems wins praise and support and will not be blamed for the situation.

↑ **Fourth** If a son unwisely tolerates inherited malpractices and tries to build upon them, he will deeply regret it.

↑ **Third** A good son must deal with troubles caused by his father: it can be no mistake, even if some pain is caused in the process.

↑ **Second** When dealing with inherited problems caused by frailty, gentleness and some tolerance are needed.

↑ **Bottom** When dealing with inherited problems, a good son will ensure that no blame falls on his father. A serious situation — but in the end good fortune will come of it.

19

Approaching

APPROACHING A CHANGE. MAKING APPROACHES.
PREPARATION.

 EARTH over LAKE suggests: The plains above a lake are blessed with great fertility.

BASIC MEANING

You should persevere in this righteous approach: it brings joy, progress and success. However, remember that summer must end in the eighth month and that things will then change for the worse.

MOVING LINES

Sixth Your approach is both humble and most generous: good fortune and absolutely no mistake.

↑ **Fifth** Your approach is wise and befits a prince: good fortune.

↑ **Fourth** You are making a perfect approach, with no mistakes.

↑ **Third** If you approach this task with complacency or over-confidence, nothing will turn out well. Some hard worrying is needed to put things right.

↑ **Second** If you approach this task together — good fortune: everything is entirely favourable.

↑ **Bottom** You should persevere in this righteous approach together: good fortune will come of it.

20

Just Looking

VIEWING. CONTEMPLATING. LOOKING BEFORE YOU LEAP.
VERSUS: TAKING A DISTORTED VIEW.

 WIND over EARTH suggests: The wind
travels everywhere but settles nowhere: it
touches everything yet grasps nothing.

BASIC MEANING

You have cleansed yourself: now think and pray before you step forward to make your offering. There is no need to hurry: sincerity and dignity in you will inspire trust and respect in others.

MOVING LINES

Sixth Unconcerned with changing circumstances, the wise man devotes himself to selfless contemplation.

↑ **Fifth** In contemplating a change in your life you will be wise to consider the needs of others.

↑ **Fourth** A visit to the king is the best way to ascertain whether you wish to serve in his kingdom.

↑ **Third** Study the course of your life to date. You will make no mistake if you base your decision to advance or retreat on past experience.

↑ **Second** You are getting a distorted view. Peeping round the door is alright for servant girls but hardly affords a balanced view.

↑ **Bottom** You are taking a childish view. Lowering yourself to peek under the door is alright for children but demeaning in people of superior abilities.

·21·

Biting Through

A Hard Solution. Judgement. Punishment.

 FIRE over THUNDER suggests: During thunder lightning must strike.

BASIC MEANING

Judgement is never pleasant – but it is necessary and will bring you success.

MOVING LINES

Sixth A hard and bitter bite. When warnings go unheeded, punishment and misfortune must follow.

↑ **Fifth** A good chew. There will be danger right to the end, so you will make no mistake to be cautious and utterly correct. There will be no error of judgement and gold will come of it.

↑ **Fourth** Gnawing the bones. A lengthy and awkward case. Arrows will be fired at you and you may even be offered bribes. If you show fortitude and utter honesty, good fortune will be yours in the end.

↑ **Third** Chewed and spat out. A case too tough to be decided. Regret, but no error of judgement.

↑ **Second** A sharp bite. An over-harsh punishment but no error of judgement.

↑ **Bottom** A nip in time. A mild preventive punishment will be no error of judgement.

22

Seeking Beauty

GRACE AND ARTISTRY.
VERSUS: VANITY AND MERE DECORATION.

 MOUNTAIN over FIRE suggests: A fire in a valley can hardly be said to illuminate the mountain.

BASIC MEANING

Seeking beauty brings success – but only if you remember that it lies in inner truth, not in decorative details. The small plans you are making at the moment will succeed well enough.

MOVING LINES

Sixth Pure simplicity is perfect beauty.

↑ **Fifth** It takes great sacrifice to reach the heights of beauty: the gift you bring is shamefully insufficient. If you persevere, however, you will succeed in the end.

↑ **Fourth** What do you want — acclaim and riches or simple tranquillity? One will rob you of your talent, the other sweetly enhance it. Surely you do not need a white horse with wings to fly out of the sky to tell you?

↑ **Third** You positively drip with talent — but it will take constant hard work to achieve success.

↑ **Second** Oh dear, what a beautiful beard! Is there anything behind it?

↑ **Bottom** Feet are beautiful — leave your carriage and walk.

23

Disintegration

SUBVERSION. STRIPPING AWAY SUPPORT. COLLAPSE.

 MOUNTAIN over EARTH suggests: A mountain collapsing into the earth.

BASIC MEANING

A time of collapse and disintegration: it is not safe to make a move of any kind.

MOVING LINES

Sixth Resist all involvement in this chaos: take no bite from this fruit. When the small and vengeful have destroyed their own dwellings, he who has remained unsullied and disinterested can win popular support and help good to return again.

↑ **Fifth** In this chaos, you seem to have some authority. The crowd follows like a fish on your line. This is highly advantageous: you can prevent excess and yet incur no resentment.

↑ **Fourth** Terrible danger is very close to you: the very cushions of the throne are being slashed and ripped apart.

↑ **Third** You cannot avoid being caught up in this turmoil — but you will not be blamed if you refuse to participate in evil or violence.

↑ **Second** The screens around the throne are being hacked to pieces. No one can be trusted now — and if you declare your loyalty to any party, you will be destroyed. Evil.

↑ **Bottom** The legs of the throne are being slowly cut away. Those loyal to the king will be destroyed. Evil.

24

Returning

TURNING BACK.

 EARTH over THUNDER suggests: Thunder underground — a warning best heeded.

BASIC MEANING

There is no harm in brief excursions – but if you decide to return, success will come of it. Friends come back to you. Even the road bends here to lead you back. In seven days a fresh start is favoured.

MOVING LINES

Sixth An evil omen. If you refuse to turn back — or turn too late — or return in disarray — if you set your armies marching in any direction whatsoever, you will meet with a terrible defeat. You will be overthrown, attacked from within as well as without — and it will take more than ten years to repair the damage.

↑ **Fifth** You won't regret it if, openly admitting your mistake, you return.

↑ **Fourth** The crowd walks on. Choosing a better way, you return alone.

↑ **Third** To keep returning to base is dangerous but necessary.

↑ **Second** Everyone welcomes your return — good fortune.

↑ **Bottom** You won't regret it if you turn back before you go too far. Indeed, great good fortune will come of it.

25

Remaining Blameless

PRESERVING INTEGRITY. RESISTING TEMPTATION.
BEHAVING HONOURABLY. AN UNEXPECTED WINDFALL.
AN UNDESERVED ACCUSATION.

 DRAGON over THUNDER suggests: A dragon should fly high — far above the thunder below.

BASIC MEANING

If you can remain entirely honest and honourable – great progress and success. If you cannot, then you will fall into deeper error and everything you undertake will end in misfortune.

MOVING LINES

Sixth Any move you make, however innocently, will bring trouble. There is nothing to be gained from any action whatsoever.

↑ **Fifth** You did nothing to bring on this illness — nor can you take any medicine to cure it: it will pass of its own accord.

↑ **Fourth** You will make no mistake to choose to remain absolutely honest.

↑ **Third** An undeserved calamity: you are unjustly accused of the theft of a cow, stolen by a passer-by.

↑ **Second** Plough your field properly, without dreaming of rich harvests. Clear the wasteland completely, without dreaming of rich fields. Advantage comes from preparing the ground correctly.

↑ **Bottom** If you start off now, openly, cheerfully and honestly, you will achieve what you aim for.

26

Building Up Power

SELF RESTRAINT.

 MOUNTAIN over DRAGON suggests: The dragon grows strong, hidden from the world in the deep chambers of his mountain home.

BASIC MEANING

Stay firmly at home for the moment, exploring your heritage of wisdom and gold, growing strong, laying great plans, developing true righteousness. Then, when the time comes to go out into the world, great good fortune will be yours, however vast your undertakings.

MOVING LINES

Sixth Great progress: the way is open and blessed and your strength is irresistible.

↑ **Fifth** This boar has impressive tusks — but if you give yourself time to geld him, he will cease to threaten you.

↑ **Fourth** Give yourself time to fix a plank to the brow of this young bull, before he grows too strong: this will prevent his horns growing and preserve your good fortune.

↑ **Third** It is valuable to band together — but beware the herd instinct. Your friends want to advance too rapidly. Restrain them. You should all practise in your chariots — and practise defensive tactics too: only then can you advance safely.

↑ **Second** You are out-numbered for the moment. No one will blame you if you wisely remove the wheels from your carts and settle down for a long wait.

↑ **Bottom** There is danger — and any further advance will expose you to it. To cease your advance now will win advantage.

27

Seeking Nourishment

SEEKING SPIRITUAL FOOD –
WHICH MAY MEAN PROVIDING NOURISHMENT FOR OTHERS.
VERSUS: GREED AND SELFISHNESS.

 MOUNTAIN over THUNDER suggests:
Thunder in the mountain valleys — a call to
silence. *Versus:* the mountain's weight
suppresses the eruption: indigestion and
stifled groans.

BASIC MEANING

Consider what nourishment you really need – and seek it;
consider what food others need – and provide it.
Moderation and insight bring good fortune.

MOVING LINES

Sixth You become a source of nourishment to others. There are dangers in such a position — but if you are aware of them, good fortune comes to all. A major journey or move will prove highly advantageous.

↑ **Fifth** You are not behaving normally or correctly at the moment: perhaps you are ill or unstable. Things will improve if you stick scrupulously to the nourishment prescribed for you — and also to what you believe to be right and honourable. Do not attempt a major journey, move or new venture.

↑ **Fourth** For you, so fierce in your pursuit of spiritual nourishment, it will be no mistake to withdraw to the mountain-top: good fortune for you — and others also.

↑ **Third** If you persist in feeding yourself these worthless sweets it will render you useless for ten years and nothing you undertake will prosper: grave misfortune.

↑ **Second** To withdraw from everyday life to seek spiritual nourishment — either in the slums with the poor or on the mountain with the sages — will bring misfortune.

↑ **Bottom** You abandon your freedom, insight and self-respect to crave enviously the food meant for another. Misfortune will come of it.

28

Excessive Weight

TOO MUCH WEIGHT. INSUFFICIENT SUPPORT.
MOUNTING PRESSURE.

 LAKE over WOOD suggests: The lake is overflowing. If the dam is not strong enough, the orchards will be drowned.

BASIC MEANING

The dam is not strong enough to support this weight of water – but if you can strengthen it, and are ready to escape to high ground if necessary, prosperity and success will come of these waters.

MOVING LINES

Sixth Struggling across a stream, a sudden flood knocks you over and sweeps you out of your depth: a dire misfortune, though you are in no way to blame.

↑ **Fifth** An old tree can still produce the odd flower: there is no harm in it, but no real value either. The same is true of an old woman and her young husband.

↑ **Fourth** Good fortune! The dam bends but with care it can hold more water yet. You would be shamefully hasty to desert it now.

↑ **Third** The dam is giving way — misfortune.

↑ **Second** There is charm and great advantage in an old tree that puts forth new shoots. Everything is entirely favourable, even for an old man and his young wife.

↑ **Bottom** You will make no mistake to acknowledge the dam's weaknesses — and plug the leaks with quite extraordinary care.

29

Danger

A Deep, Dark Pit.

 WATER over *WATER* suggests: A chasm in a chasm — danger within danger.

BASIC MEANING

If you are alert, true-hearted and confident, you can steer through this perilous chasm and survive.

MOVING LINES

Sixth You are shamefully bound and then imprisoned in a thorn thicket. No pardon or escape looks possible for three years: an evil plight.

↑ **Fifth** You will not drown in this pit: the water will not rise further and the danger can be overcome if you act sensibly.

↑ **Fourth** You are trapped in this pit. Do not hesitate to call for help — for this catastrophe is not your fault and at least food and drink will be passed in to you.

↑ **Third** Great danger ahead and great danger behind — but do not move, or you will fall into the deepest pit of the abyss.

↑ **Second** The steep walls of this chasm are most dangerous. You should not try to escape in one bold rush: try to withdraw cautiously, winning yourself time to breathe and to plan the next safe step.

↑ **Bottom** Danger within danger: lost in a chasm, you miss the path and fall into a crevasse — an evil plight.

30

Warmth

AFFECTION. BEAUTY. RADIANCE.

 FIRE over FIRE suggests: Fire light and fire bright, warmly glowing through the night.

BASIC MEANING

Consistently support those who depend on you – and gratefully welcome their help to you. Such affectionate persistence leads to success and good fortune.

MOVING LINES

Sixth You lead your people to brilliant victory, avoid excessive punishments, are tolerant to those led into evil by others: this is indeed enlightened behaviour.

↑ **Fifth** Enlightened, you shed tears of grief and repentance. This shows progress and therefore leads to good fortune.

↑ **Fourth** A rick bursts suddenly into flame: it blazes to heaven, dies down — and is abandoned.

↑ **Third** It is beautiful and natural for the sun to sink — but it is an omen of misfortune for those who bitterly lament their age, or drunkenly howl defiant songs.

↑ **Second** Golden sunlight: great good fortune.

↑ **Bottom** Dawn: minor mistakes will not matter if you are reverent and respectful in your approach.

31

Attraction

SUPPORTIVE INFLUENCE. COMPLEMENTARY QUALITIES.
COURTSHIP.

 LAKE over MOUNTAIN suggests: A pool on a mountain: if the combination is to be perfect, the pool will beautify the mountain and the mountain will support the pool.

BASIC MEANING

However attracted, it is wise not to seduce nor be seduced. You will enjoy success and happiness if you put another's feelings and needs before your own. Marriage is favoured, especially if a young girl is involved.

MOVING LINES

Sixth A twitching tongue signifies that you talk too much and achieve nothing.

↑ **Fifth** Shivers down the spine signify attraction without action — and no regrets, either.

↑ **Fourth** Rapid heartbeats signify that you are torn between two impulses — and whatever you decide is likely to happen. If you decide to be scrupulously virtuous, fair and sensitive to others, good fortune will follow — and the possibility of losing a friend will disappear.

↑ **Third** Tingling thighs signify that you cling too hard to someone. There will be shame and misfortune if you continue to depend in this way.

↑ **Second** Tapping feet signify that you have an irresistible urge to advance — but misfortune will follow if you do. Curb this impulse: to pause will bring good fortune.

↑ **Bottom** Twitching toes signify that you are in a state of excitement — but isn't this too exciting and worrying, too far beyond you . . .?

32

Loyalty

Stability. Perseverance in a Long-Lasting Situation.

 THUNDER over WIND suggests: Brief thunder overhead: the wind that brought it goes on and on.

BASIC MEANING

Stability brings prosperity and success. You will make no mistake, therefore, if you loyally maintain the present situation. There is certainly advantage in going ahead with plans – but not in changing your basic pattern.

MOVING LINES

Sixth This continued restlessness can achieve nothing: indeed, it will bring misfortune.

↑ **Fifth** To be endlessly loyal and submissive becomes some wives — but it brings misfortune to a man of affairs.

↑ **Fourth** You continue to hunt in the wrong field.

↑ **Third** If you have not been consistently loyal, disgrace may occur. To continue such behaviour will bring lasting humiliation.

↑ **Second** Situation stable: these sorrows cannot last.

↑ **Bottom** To take hasty action is not the way to secure a stable future: nothing advantageous can come of it.

· 33 ·

Retreat

<small>STRATEGIC WITHDRAWAL. YIELDING. RETIREMENT.</small>

 DRAGON over MOUNTAIN suggests: The dragon withdraws to his mountain top.

BASIC MEANING

A controlled retreat now – with every detail meticulously worked out – will lead to success in the end.

MOVING LINES

Sixth You retire gladly, to well-earned ease: everything is entirely favourable.

↑ **Fifth** You are right to make a controlled retreat. It requires great care but will lead to good fortune.

↑ **Fourth** There is good reason for retreat. The wise man will acknowledge this — and succeed in the end; the fool will refuse to retreat — and meet misfortune.

↑ **Third** In the middle of a forced retreat it is terribly dangerous and nerve-wracking to halt — but you will succeed in saving the women and servants if you wait for them.

↑ **Second** Refusing to retreat, he has lashed himself to his post with rawhide ropes. No one can make him budge.

↑ **Bottom** If you retreat too far, the situation will become even more perilous. Make no further move in any direction.

34

Justified Action

THE POWER OF RIGHTEOUSNESS. SHOWING YOUR STRENGTH.

 THUNDER over DRAGON suggests: The dragon's roar fills the sky with thunder.

BASIC MEANING

To move persistently forward in this righteous course will bring advantage.

MOVING LINES

Sixth The ram that catches his horns in a hedge cannot advance and cannot retreat. Nothing is favourable — except to recognize the danger of this predicament and keep out of it. Once in it, you must simply endure.

↑ **Fifth** Forget that rams charge madly about — sit down and enjoy this lush pasture. You won't regret it.

↑ **Fourth** You can break through this hedge and its entanglements if you remember that your cart depends on its weight and the quiet strength of its axle, not on the noisy rattle of its wheels. Persist in this righteous endeavour: you will find good fortune and worries will be left behind.

↑ **Third** A small, mean-minded goat will charge at a hedge again and again — until his horns get hopelessly entangled. You will be wise not to behave like this but to conserve your energy and refrain from action.

↑ **Second** If you move straight ahead along this righteous path you will find good fortune.

↑ **Bottom** Stamping your hoof and pawing the ground is merely exhausting — and an actual charge will bring grave misfortune.

35

Seeking Reward

STILL TRYING TO MAKE PROGRESS.

 FIRE over EARTH suggests: The fires of the procession twinkle across the plain.

BASIC MEANING

Having done much for his people, the prince is granted audience three times and receives many helpful gifts. Note that these gifts are not necessarily what he asks for – and that there is no mention of good fortune or ultimate success.

MOVING LINES

Sixth You are right to be wary as you advance – but take care that you lower your horns only against rebels in your own city: here a brief show of strength will bring good fortune. To show your horns for too long or to the wrong people, however, will bring shame and deep regret.

↑ **Fifth** Don't concern yourself with gain or loss – just advance: everything is favourable and your worries will vanish.

↑ **Fourth** Stop this jittering: running forwards then backwards, like a squirrel, will lead to misfortune.

↑ **Third** Everyone is in accord. Progress can be made and worry vanishes.

↑ **Second** You progress – but in sorrow: scrupulous sensitivity and honesty are needful. You will benefit greatly from help given by an elderly person, probably female, who is important to you.

↑ **Bottom** If your progress is frustrated – persist. If people do not trust you, do not let this upset your generosity and tolerance towards them: they will see their error and good fortune will come of it.

36

Darkening of the Light

DELIBERATE INJURY. DARKNESS. ECLIPSE.

 EARTH over FIRE suggests: Earth thrown on a fire; warmth and light are quenched.

BASIC MEANING

In great darkness, remain true. Dawn will come again.

MOVING LINES

Sixth To fall from such a great height gives no chance of recovery: the light has gone and there is utter darkness. The only consolation is that darkness, too, must pass in the end.

↑ **Fifth** However dark it becomes, remain true and at your post.

↑ **Fourth** Creeping into the enemy camp, you come close to the very source of darkness. Its unpleasant nature leaves you no hope of mercy: it is wisest to abandon what cannot be saved.

↑ **Third** It is reckless to pursue the dark enemy into the night, his own domain. Although you catch up with him it is you who are wounded — and this foray is unlikely to improve things at all.

↑ **Second** Grievously wounded, you have held out until sunset. Now the light fades — and a strong horse will carry you to safety.

↑ **Bottom** Wherever you fly, you cannot escape the fading of the light. Your wings droop and for three days you have no chance to eat. Wherever you go you are derided and receive no help.

37

Family Concerns

 WOOD over FIRE suggests: A fire in a hut: warmth and security.

BASIC MEANING

Fulfill your correct family role. Patience and loyalty at home will bring advantage to all members of the family.

MOVING LINES

Sixth You do not realize how frightening and unapproachable you seem to your family. Think about it and adjust. Good fortune will come of it, though it may take a long time.

↑ **Fifth** A good king rules his family with kindness *and* severity — and so must you. There is no need to worry about it. Good fortune will come of it.

↑ **Fourth** Great good fortune: the family is significantly enriched — perhaps by the addition of a daughter or wife, a real treasure.

↑ **Third** When tempers flare or a punishment is over-severe, there can be a nasty moment in a family. But afterwards, everyone is sorry and the air is cleared — a good outcome. However, if women and children choose to giggle disrespectfully at this moment, misfortune will follow.

↑ **Second** You should abandon these distractions and attend to the kitchen and your family duties. Nothing else can bring good fortune.

↑ **Bottom** You should establish firm rules in your home — then this unhappiness will vanish.

38

Estrangement

DISAGREEMENT. SEPARATION. ISOLATION.

 FIRE over LAKE suggests: A fire on a lake seems impossible — until you look at a sunset across the water.

BASIC MEANING

Estrangement is serious: while it lasts there can be success only in small matters. Take small steps, therefore, towards the warmth and joy of reconciliation.

MOVING LINES

Sixth Feeling isolated and oppressed you see even your best friend as a pig or a demon: you even go to shoot him. But lay your bow aside — this is clearly not a robber but someone who will love you if you let him. Tears will bring you together and reconciliation will bring good fortune.

↑ **Fifth** Someone is taking steps to end this feud. If only you will take a step towards him, reconciliation will bring great rejoicing.

↑ **Fourth** You are in an unpleasant position. But though you feel alone and isolated, you will soon meet a true fellow-spirit, someone to trust and collaborate with.

↑ **Third** Horses halted in front; carriage boarded from behind — they must be bandits! They shave your head; they cut off your nose. A rough beginning but it won't last long and, astonishingly, the final outcome will not be bad.

↑ **Second** To meet your lord in a back alley will prove quite correct.

↑ **Bottom** It is wise not to follow the horses you have lost: they will return of their own accord. It is wise not to ignore evil people: see them, but do not deal with them. Acting in these ways, your distress will vanish.

39

Meeting an Obstacle

A MAJOR DIFFICULTY.

 CHASM over MOUNTAIN suggests: A crevasse in the mountains, hard and dangerous to pass.

BASIC MEANING

A major obstacle ahead! Retreat is favoured, for advance seems perilous. Don't give up, however: good fortune will follow if you think hard, take advice and carefully select a safer route.

MOVING LINES

Sixth To proceed will lead to greater danger. Good fortune will result if you turn back and take wise advice.

↑ **Fifth** The difficulties are immense — but friends are coming. Hold on!

↑ **Fourth** To proceed will lead to greater danger — therefore turn back and seek reliable helpers.

↑ **Third** To proceed will lead to greater danger — therefore turn back to your friends and womenfolk.

↑ **Second** Problem follows problem — but they are not your own, nor are you to blame.

↑ **Bottom** To proceed will lead to difficulty. To wait or turn back will win praise.

40

Liberation

RELIEF. RELEASE. DELIVERANCE.

 THUNDER over WATER suggests: Beating our drums, we ride to freedom out of the gorge.

BASIC MEANING

If liberation is to be achieved, action must be undertaken at once. When liberation comes, restoring former, familiar conditions brings good fortune.

MOVING LINES

Sixth From the very top of a high tower, the prince shoots down a falcon. Seeing this, the rebels flee. The effect is therefore liberating and entirely advantageous.

↑ **Fifth** Setting himself free, the truly great person achieves good fortune. Lesser people retire, dismayed.

↑ **Fourth** Free yourself from this dependence: new and trustworthy friends will appear.

↑ **Third** If a peasant persists in riding out in his new carriage he will cause resentment, tempt robbers to attack him and suffer humiliation in the end.

↑ **Second** Perseverance in the hunt brings good fortune. You catch three foxes and emerge to win the golden arrow.

↑ **Bottom** No blame. No mistake.

41

Reduction

MAKING REDUCTIONS. REDUCED CIRCUMSTANCES. DECREASE.

 MOUNTAIN over LAKE suggests: In summer the mountain sheds its waters, replenishing the lake below.

BASIC MEANING

Great good fortune will come if you choose to make deliberate, conscious reductions. It is certainly not a mistake. Indeed, it will be advantageous to start at once and to persevere in this course. However, do not empty your own bowl to over-fill another's: let both bowls contain enough rice.

MOVING LINES

Sixth If you gain without depriving others, there can be no blame. Go ahead — but take care to be absolutely fair and correct. You will gain supporters, though not among your family.

↑ **Fifth** Immense good fortune: people shower you with riches and will take no refusal.

↑ **Fourth** Illness and distressing problems will be reduced if you seek help quickly. No one will think the worse of you for asking — and help will be gladly given.

↑ **Third** When three people go travelling together, one is likely to leave the group. A person travelling alone, however, is likely to find a companion.

↑ **Second** You are able to bring increase to others without significantly decreasing your own. Persevere in this plan but take care: any action taken now will bring misfortune. Give more thought to the fairest way to do it.

↑ **Bottom** You are right to leave this work and hurry away. But don't be too hasty: consider carefully how much you can leave behind and whether others will lose by your action.

42

Expansion

GAIN. GROWTH. ENRICHMENT. INCREASE.

 WOOD over THUNDER suggests:
Thunder at the root of a fruit tree:
exceptional growth this summer.

BASIC MEANING

This is a favourable time for undertaking great tasks, even significant journeys and moves.

MOVING LINES

Sixth Your plans are selfish and ill-worked-out. They will not find support and are likely to be bitterly opposed. Misfortune.

↑ **Fifth** Your generosity is recognized and appreciated: you hardly need to ask permission to go ahead. Great good fortune will come of this project.

↑ **Fourth** Your sound and philanthropic advice will be followed. Indeed, you will be entrusted with large tasks of removal and re-organization — and great gain will come of this.

↑ **Third** To avoid blame, be especially open and informative now. Although you are in no way at fault, you are likely to be enriched because of unfortunate events.

↑ **Second** To persevere in what you know is right will bring good fortune. Indeed, great enrichment will come to you unexpectedly and can hardly be declined.

↑ **Bottom** This period is highly favourable for undertaking great tasks: you will make no mistake and great success will come of it.

43

Resolute Reform

DEFENDING WHAT IS GOOD. REMOVING BAD INFLUENCES.

 LAKE over DRAGON suggests: The dragon plunges to clear the spring, choked by weeds beneath the lake.

BASIC MEANING

Bring truth to light – but expect danger.
Be strong – but seek support. Be resolute – but always peaceful.
Advance – but cautiously.

MOVING LINES

Sixth In this struggle you have no friends to call out to for help: misfortune in the end.

↑ **Fifth** The small and mean should be uprooted with determination, like weeds sprouting in the shadows. However, if you are to avoid blame and a possible error, you must allow their unpleasantness to become apparent before you take action.

↑ **Fourth** You won't get hurt if you stay with your companions — but you will learn a crippling lesson if you attempt the struggle alone. Alas, you are unlikely to heed this advice.

↑ **Third** If, as seems likely, the coming advance is made too boldly, there will be grave misfortune. Therefore you will make no mistake to stay behind, alone, unsheltered and suffering the scorn of others. In the end you will be seen to have been wise.

↑ **Second** Be watchful: warn your friends: seek their support. Then there will be no need to worry, even if a night attack is made upon you.

↑ **Bottom** To make this great show of strength is an error: you cannot win this struggle.

44

Being Carried Away

BEING INFLUENCED UNWISELY.
AN INVITATION FROM A WOMAN.

 DRAGON over WIND suggests: A dragon mounted on the wind yields up all power.

BASIC MEANING

Invitations seem delightful – but often they merely tempt or mislead. You should not marry on the strength of this offer.

MOVING LINES

Sixth You may be right to be careful but you will sorely regret it if you lower your horns too far: someone approaching you in friendship will get hurt or driven away.

↑ **Fifth** Melons grow best in the shade. Keep this seedling out of the sun: blessings will come of it.

↑ **Fourth** You keep no fish in your fishtank, nor provisions for guests. Misfortune.

↑ **Third** This is dangerous. But the hide has been tanned from your bottom once, so perhaps you'll have the sense not to get flayed again.

↑ **Second** Quite correct: you have a fish in the fishtank and provisions in the larder — but you don't offer them to these guests.

↑ **Bottom** Tie yourself down! You are behaving like a starved pig and only enforced restraint can bring good fortune. To let this passion take its course will bring disaster.

45

Mingling

GETTING TOGETHER. A GATHERING.

 LAKE over EARTH suggests: Where many waters mingle on the plain a lake is formed, bringing joy to all.

BASIC MEANING

It is good to gather together with your family – or, indeed, with any other group. Prosperity and success will come of this gathering, especially if you are well-behaved, show filial respect and seek guidance from an elder person. Perhaps this will help you find a purpose you seem to lack. However, be prepared for a surprise or a shock.

MOVING LINES

Sixth There will be grief and mourning at this gathering – but no mistakes.

↑ **Fifth** You are in a position to bring people together – and you should do so. You may not be trusted at first, but if you persevere, your good intentions will become clear and worry and unhappiness will cease.

↑ **Fourth** Great good fortune will come of this gathering: just take care to behave impeccably.

↑ **Third** Even in company, you sigh for companionship. Nothing seems to help you. If some sort of promotion is offered, you will be wise to accept it, despite your doubts or regrets.

↑ **Second** You will make no mistake in letting yourself be drawn into this group – indeed, it will bring you good fortune. It will help if you make an offering of some sort: its size doesn't matter – it is the sincerity of the gift that counts.

↑ **Bottom** You seem confused and indecisive, sincerely wanting to be part of a gathering – and then running away from it. Don't be upset: ask openly for help and advice: it will be given, clarifying everything. Your sadness will turn to laughter, once everything is clear – for even if you decide against the gathering, no one will blame you.

· 46 ·

Striving Upwards

ASCENDING. TRANSCENDING. SEEKING PROMOTION.

 EARTH over WOOD suggests: Rising through the earth — seed, sapling, soon the sky.

BASIC MEANING

Don't be anxious: striving upwards brings great progress and supreme success. However, it is wise to seek the guidance of a great man and never to cease in your endeavour.

MOVING LINES

Sixth What is gained by climbing at night is likely to be lost with a fall. You will find more advantage in daytime vigilance and scrupulously correct behaviour.

↑ **Fifth** You are rising steadily and sensibly, step by step. Persevere on this course and you will succeed triumphantly.

↑ **Fourth** It is no mistake to have faith in ancient traditions; they will bring good fortune and reward.

↑ **Third** It is easy to become lord of an empty city. Have no doubts and do not hesitate for there is no one to challenge you.

↑ **Second** Your faith is well-founded and will yield true happiness.

↑ **Bottom** Everyone warmly approves your growth: promotion and great good fortune are certain.

47

Exhaustion

ADVERSITY. OPPRESSION. DISABLEMENT. DEPRESSION.

 LAKE over CHASM suggests: A chasm opens underneath a lake: loss of all water.

BASIC MEANING

Arguing and pleading seem useless: no one hears you; no one believes you. In this plight, only the truly great can remain both blameless and unbowed – but if you can, then you may still turn this adversity into success.

MOVING LINES

Sixth Entangled by a few thorns, you seem scared that it will hurt you to break free — and over-concerned about your past misdemeanours. Don't be foolish: if you sincerely repent and make determined efforts to free yourself, good fortune will come of all this in the end.

↑ **Fifth** If there is to be a solution, you will not find it on the road you are following now: here there is trouble with an overlord, so severe that your nose and feet are cut off. Prayer and sacrifice are needed if this is to be averted.

↑ **Fourth** You have the means in abundance — but you seem to lack all will to do what you should. Shame on you! But you will come to your senses before long.

↑ **Third** You sought shelter among rocks, with thorns and thistles your only bed. Now, going home, you cannot find your wife: an evil plight.

↑ **Second** When fine food and drink, even a coming high position, cannot cheer you — prayer and sacrifice are what is needed. To start any new venture in this frame of mind will bring misfortune. You will make no mistake to pray for more cheerfulness and more patience.

↑ **Bottom** You have led yourself into a dark valley and are entangled in dry, thorny undergrowth. It will be three years before you see the light and find deliverance.

48

Thirst at the Well

POSSIBLE REFRESHMENT. PROBABLE FRUSTRATION.

 CHASM over WOOD suggests: A bucket in a well. It can provide refreshment and indeed life. But when the rope is broken and the bucket lost — thirst.

BASIC MEANING

The water in this well endures for ever while those who use it rise and fall, succeed and fail, come and pass away. If your rope is too short or your bucket leaks you will find frustration here.

MOVING LINES

Sixth This well is full to the top and you may use it freely — great good fortune.

↑ **Fifth** Cool and clean, the water in this well is excellent to drink.

↑ **Fourth** This well needs repair but you are right to believe that it will yield water.

↑ **Third** They started to dig this well but never reached the water. Sad, for we know it is there and we could all have used it if our ruler had only dug deeper.

↑ **Second** This well has leaked its water away. Your bucket leaks too. You can get only a trickle here.

↑ **Bottom** The water in this well is muddy and undrinkable: even the birds no longer visit it.

49

Revolution

SLOUGHING ONE'S SKIN. DRASTIC REFORM.
FUNDAMENTAL CHANGE.

 LAKE over FIRE suggests: When volcanic fire bursts upward, the crater lake is blasted into vapour.

BASIC MEANING

When the time is ripe, you yourself – perhaps to your amazement – can make a necessary change happen. Persevere and it will come, bringing supreme success and an end to all sadness.

MOVING LINES

Sixth Reforms made now with the subtle smoothness of a panther will inspire admiration and docility. The jackals will switch allegiance and follow you. After the big change, further advances will prove unfortunate. If you seek only to stabilise the situation good fortune will result.

↑ **Fifth** Reforms made now with the strength and bravery of a tiger will inspire trust, admiration and obedience.

↑ **Fourth** At last people believe you. Impediments disappear and your reforming action will lead to good fortune.

↑ **Third** To take action now will bring trouble — and persistent attempts will be most dangerous. You must discuss this reform at least three times: only then will people believe you and give you the backing you need before you take action.

↑ **Second** When the time is ripe, reforming action will prove successful. You will make no mistake to start it soon.

↑ **Bottom** You are bound with raw-hide bonds. As you cannot yet take the reforming action that is needed, don't try: you can only exhaust yourself.

50

A Cauldron of Emotion

TRANSFORMING WHAT IT COOKS. A SACRIFICE.

 FIRE over WIND suggests: A cooking pot on an open fire can spill or spoil when the wind rises.

BASIC MEANING

Something you dearly love must be sacrificed. You cannot feel it now, but supreme good fortune, progress and prosperity will result.

MOVING LINES

Sixth The gift of this cauldron with jade handles is a princely reward: it signifies great good fortune — everything is entirely favourable.

↑ **Fifth** A cauldron may have elaborate golden handles — but it is useful only if it cooks well. It will prove advantageous to be thrifty, sensible and austere.

↑ **Fourth** The cauldron's legs break: the prince's food is spilled and his fine clothes ruined. Trust evaporates. There is shame and bitter misfortune.

↑ **Third** How foolish to cook in a cauldron that has no handles: it can't be lifted, so all that delicious food is wasted and useless. However, this mistake will be forgiven and forgotten and in the end good fortune will come of it.

↑ **Second** Your cauldron has good, solid food in it. Others are envious — but if you are careful, their spite won't affect you. Good fortune!

↑ **Bottom** You will be wise to tip this cauldron right over, tipping out its unwholesome contents. There is no shame in it, just as there can be no shame in openly taking a wife to give her a home and yourself children.

51

Turbulence

An Earthquake. Shock. Arousement.

 THUNDER over THUNDER suggests: Thunder underground and thunder overhead — what a storm!

BASIC MEANING

Thunder comes, bringing terror to all. Bow down in awe before this storm – but do not flinch. If the wine remains unspilt in your glass, laughter, elation and success will follow.

MOVING LINES

Sixth A terrifying earthquake brings ruin and rumour. It is not your fault that the danger seems more to others than to you — and that it affects them first. Don't panic — and don't move, or great misfortune will befall you.

↑ **Fifth** Earth tremors all around: people run hither and thither, though it is most dangerous to move. With careful thought and quick reactions you should be able to save your belongings.

↑ **Fourth** During earthquakes all paths are treacherous with mud.

↑ **Third** An earthquake seems to rob you of your senses — but if you are startled into dramatic action it is likely to prove correct and fruitful.

↑ **Second** A dangerous earthquake is coming. Don't worry about your treasured possessions: leave them and climb to safety in the hills. Don't attempt to recover your belongings: you will get them back in seven days.

↑ **Bottom** A brief earthquake: after the initial shock, you laugh and cheer. Good fortune!

52

Stillness

DESISTING. STAYING PUT. NO CHANGE.
SPIRITUAL SILENCE.
VERSUS: OBSTINATE IMMOVABILITY.

 MOUNTAIN over MOUNTAIN suggests:
Rock upon rock: silence and stillness.

BASIC MEANING

Silently rest. When all self-interest is abandoned, action is as blameless as inaction. Peace.

MOVING LINES

Sixth To seek tranquillity of spirit is the noblest search, to find it the greatest blessing: good fortune!

↑ **Fifth** You will improve matters if you say nothing or speak only after deep consideration.

↑ **Fourth** You will make no mistake if you seek to calm yourself with conscious meditation.

↑ **Third** This situation is thrilling but perilous. Restrain yourself, but not too harshly, for it can be dangerous to smother natural affections and appetites.

↑ **Second** People will not turn back to listen to your advice. Sadly, you should cease your vain attempts to save them.

↑ **Bottom** If you remain firmly in your present correct position, you will make no mistake. Resist all temptations to move, even an inch.

53

Growing Slowly

 WOOD over MOUNTAIN suggests: A tree on a mountaintop: slowly it grows.

BASIC MEANING

A good relationship grows slowly, step by careful step. However, if you go too slowly it will become stunted. Therefore actively develop co-operation and draw up firm plans and guidelines for your partnership: then lasting good fortune, freedom and position will result.

MOVING LINES

Sixth Wings slowly beating, the geese fly over the mountains and away. The sky is their true home: its achievement brings good fortune to all. Even the feathers that they leave behind are sacred.

↑ **Fifth** For three years the goose has clambered over the hills, seeking a perfect hillock for her nest. In the end she finds everything her heart desires: incomparable good fortune.

↑ **Fourth** The geese are slowly circling a tree – a safe but unsuitable perch for a goose. If they can find a flat, spreading branch they may be able to alight and perch safely.

↑ **Third** The geese have gradually strayed into an arid plain. They should stay together, for they may have to fight off predators. If the male goes out to forage, he may fail to return. As for the female, a cherished project may be stillborn or have to be delayed.

↑ **Second** A pair of geese walk cautiously into the shelter of the rocks. Here they can eat and drink, happily at peace among the flock. Good fortune.

↑ **Bottom** With her friends, the young goose paddles cautiously in towards the shore. She may hear gossip or rumours about a youngster in trouble but he is in fact blameless and her trust in him is correct.

54

Planning a Marriage

A PLAN NOT SOUNDLY BASED.
A MARRIAGE UNLIKELY TO OCCUR –
OR DOOMED TO UNHAPPINESS.

 THUNDER over LAKE suggests: Thunder on high. The lake trembles but cannot follow.

BASIC MEANING

Any action will bring misfortune. There is really nothing favourable in this plan.

MOVING LINES

Sixth A loveless match of empty formality: nothing can go right in such a marriage.

↑ **Fifth** Good fortune! The bride dresses modestly for her husband's sake. Her friends and bridesmaids are far more splendid.

↑ **Fourth** It is wiser to marry late than to make a mistake. She has already waited far longer than is usual but in the end she will marry.

↑ **Third** This marriage can rescue you from servitude but it will not give you the respect, affection or fulfilment you desire.

↑ **Second** Though you can see, it is not good to have one blind eye. In this marriage you are left alone and can do little more than preserve appearances.

↑ **Bottom** Though you can walk, it is not good to be lame. Though you marry, it is not good to find other women in your husband's house. Go ahead into this good fortune but remember that it may not be as good as you think.

· 55 ·

Abundance

FULFILMENT. HARVEST. DAZZLING CONTRAST.
SPECTACULAR PHENOMENA.

 THUNDER over FIRE suggests: Thunder at noon: the sky darkens but lightning illuminates the golden corn below.

BASIC MEANING

Do not be troubled by your prosperity. Use your position, share your riches and enjoy your prominence while it lasts.

MOVING LINES

Sixth Great misfortune and loneliness will haunt you if you stake too much on material prosperity. What use is a large and splendid house if you lose your family and friends to build it . . .?

↑ **Fifth** The thunder passes. You attract people of great and shining ability to your cause: blessings, acclaim and good fortune.

↑ **Fourth** An immense darkness at noon: the sun looks like a distant star. But when you meet your destined partner — almost a soul-mate, a person of equal rank, ability and interest to yourself — then action may be taken and good fortune will come of it.

↑ **Third** An immense darkness and cloudburst at noon. In the darkness you break your right arm. There can be no blame and much wisdom in postponing all great tasks for the moment.

↑ **Second** An immense darkness at high noon: the sun looks like a distant star. While it lasts, any action you take will arouse suspicion and resentment. Do nothing, therefore, except build confidence by showing how much you care for the harvest: this will lead to good fortune in the end.

↑ **Bottom** You meet a destined partner — almost a soul-mate, a person of equal rank, ability and interests as yourself. A long period of working together, possibly in his/her realm, is highly productive but troubles may follow if this splendid period is extended beyond its natural term. Much progress in winning respect is made at this time.

· 56 ·

Wandering

Seeking.

 FIRE over MOUNTAIN suggests: A traveller's fire on top of a mountain, here today and gone tomorrow.

BASIC MEANING

You may enjoy these incidental wanderings but this is not your real quest, nor this inn your real home.

MOVING LINES

Sixth This inn is not safe. The traveller may laugh out loud to begin with but then misfortune afflicts him too. He will lose his horses and sleep in the field.

↑ **Fifth** Risking an arrow, the traveller shoots down a pheasant with his first shot. This wins him work and a certain local renown.

↑ **Fourth** A traveller finds shelter and work of a sort but he does not feel safe here, nor happy, nor at ease.

↑ **Third** Somehow the traveller causes fire at the inn. He loses the trust of his travelling companions. To continue the journey would be very dangerous.

↑ **Second** Good fortune! The traveller has money in his pocket and is made welcome at the inn. He even finds a trustworthy companion for the road.

↑ **Bottom** A traveller who is mean or over-inquisitive soon exhausts his welcome: calamity.

57

Dedication

GENTLE PERSISTENCE AND EFFECTIVENESS.
VERSUS: TIMIDITY. INDECISION.

 WIND over WIND suggests: The wind in the woods: a gentle rustling.

BASIC MEANING

Gentleness makes gentle progress and perhaps this is enough for you? You can achieve more if you explore comprehensively, define your goal firmly, seek advice and consciously move forward. Be more confident, for the winds are favourable.

MOVING LINES

Sixth A dying wind. This fear and weakness will not do — they bring certain misfortune. You will lose all ability to defend yourself, and lose your property too.

↑ **Fifth** Strong wind rising and changing to a settled course. A weak beginning but a splendid end. Good fortune comes now, with a major change — but think about it for three days before you act, and keep on looking for improvements.

↑ **Fourth** Strong, steady breeze. All sadness blows away. Three kinds of game are caught in a glorious hunt.

↑ **Third** Feeble puffs of wind. To attempt something half-heartedly, over and over again, simply brings humiliation.

↑ **Second** A restless wind. What do you fear? There is no need to consult all these fortune-tellers and magicians: you are on the right course and good fortune will result if you stick to it.

↑ **Bottom** Light and changeable winds. Don't be hesitant. Whether you decide to advance or retreat, plan hard, pay full attention to detail, don't be over-gentle and don't give up.

58

Truth

JOY. FRIENDSHIP. PURITY.

 LAKE over LAKE suggests: Unusual depth and unusual clarity.

BASIC MEANING

Truth and true friends – two joys that bring delight and success.

MOVING LINES

Sixth Pleasure and pleasure-seeking friends will lure you away from real joy.

↑ **Fifth** Watch out! You are placing your trust in a friend who is not trustworthy and will cause you distress.

↑ **Fourth** Joy is peace: you can't find it by mathematics or by jumping from one pleasure to another. Give up these experiments before they damage you: then true joy will arise of its own accord.

↑ **Third** Joy cannot be sought. To seek it brings misfortune.

↑ **Second** Truth and joy go hand-in-hand. You are right — so don't worry: be confident and enjoy the good fortune such confidence brings.

↑ **Bottom** Joy and good fortune! You are content and therefore in harmony with everything.

·59·

Dispersion

SCATTERING OF A GROUP. DISSOLUTION OF AN INSTITUTION.
SELFLESSNESS. DISSOLVING DIFFERENCES.

 WIND over CHASM suggests: A breeze can lift the waters from a gorge: rising as mist it blows away.

BASIC MEANING

If you wish your troubles to dissolve, you must melt too. Peace and reunion come only to the selfless. Important decisions and journeys will succeed now – but only if you seek the greater good, the good of all.

MOVING LINES

Sixth Strife and pain will vanish away if you remove yourself to a safe distance and refuse to be involved.

↑ **Fifth** Fever is cured by sweating. Similarly, a fever in the state can be safely cured if the king publicly shares out its wealth among the people.

↑ **Fourth** It is hard to believe it – but if you break up your group and disperse your companions now, both friends and good fortune will come back in even greater abundance.

↑ **Third** When all selfishness melts away and one works entirely for others, personal sadness cannot remain.

↑ **Second** When things disintegrate around you, cling to what you love most – to God and the family. Then your distress will seem less important.

↑ **Bottom** Help given to and by others will provide the strength to escape from evil. Good fortune and safety.

·60·

Limitation

Severe Restriction. Reaching the Limit.

 WATER over LAKE suggests: A lake in a chasm, hemmed in and unable to spread.

BASIC MEANING

To gladly set or accept limits to your power will bring success.
However, to accept harsh limitations laid upon you by others
would be disastrous – and to inflict repressive limitations on
yourself is equally unwise.

MOVING LINES

Sixth If you accept or impose harsh restrictions for too long, great misfortune will come of it. Unhappiness will disappear only if you resolutely quit this situation.

↑ **Fifth** Voluntarily to limit your own power brings good fortune. To go further and to give up position and possessions will bring acclaim.

↑ **Fourth** Success and prosperity will come of these restrictions and limitations.

↑ **Third** If you set no limit to your activities you will have cause to lament. You are doing too much. Though no one will blame you for a misfortune, it can be avoided.

↑ **Second** To lock yourself up in your own room is a foolish limitation. You will miss an opportunity and deeply regret it.

↑ **Bottom** You will make no mistake to remain at home, limiting yourself to activities within your own fields.

61

Serenity Within

SECURITY. CONFIDENCE. GOOD INFLUENCE ON OTHERS.

 WIND over LAKE suggests: The freshness of the lake rises to scent the wind.

BASIC MEANING

Cling firmly to what you believe. Then your sincerity will successfully influence everyone, even the most intractable opposition. A journey or move or important decision can successfully be made at this time of serene self-confidence.

MOVING LINES

Sixth The village cocks crow loudly — the alarm! Disaster will follow if you continue to ignore them.

↑ **Fifth** Serene and sure he steps through the marshes. The other cranes follow, safely and happily.

↑ **Fourth** When the moon is nearly full we let our horses run loose in the marshes. Wherever they wander, no harm can befall them.

↑ **Third** Good comrades share the battle as well as days of peace. Good comrades share the tears as well as the laughter and music.

↑ **Second** The crane calls from the shade and its young answer happily, 'This is the life! Let us share it together!'

↑ **Bottom** A heron fishing: he makes no plans but nothing distracts him. He is fully prepared but fully relaxed. Good fortune is certain.

62

Safety in Smallness

LYING LOW. ATTENTION TO DETAIL.

 THUNDER over MOUNTAIN suggests:
When thunder fills the sky, wise birds seek
shelter on the mountain.

BASIC MEANING

In changeable weather birds who fly too high may perish, while those who seek shelter sing happily. Be exceptionally cautious and conscientious now for small affairs are blessed with good fortune, while greater ones may prove most dangerous.

MOVING LINES

Sixth The storm has almost passed overhead. To leave shelter now, or to fly away will bring real misfortune — a self-inflicted injury.

↑ **Fifth** Those thunderclouds are too high and too far to threaten a storm. There is no need to hide — and hunters may all-too-easily shoot a bird hiding in a cave.

↑ **Fourth** The storm will pass overhead: do not attempt to confront it. To leave your nest brings danger. Be on your guard and do nothing positive for a long time.

↑ **Third** Beware! If you are not extremely careful someone may creep up behind and strike you down.

↑ **Second** Don't fly so high! However hard you try you will not reach the King — and should be satisfied with meeting his official (who may be a woman).

↑ **Bottom** Wherever it flies now, the bird meets with misfortune.

63

Completion – And After

 WATER over FIRE suggests: A cauldron boiling on the fire for a celebration feast.

BASIC MEANING

All seems successfully resolved – but take great care. A brief success is not a final victory and further confusion could easily follow. This pot will boil dry or spill, without great diligence and firmly honourable conduct.

MOVING LINES

Sixth Take care! To dip your head too deep in the wine jar will bring real danger and trouble upon you.

↑ **Fifth** A small but appropriate offering, given at the right time, brings more good fortune than a large or showy one, wrongly timed.

↑ **Fourth** Be careful. The finest clothes can turn to rags. Though you celebrate, dissatisfied people are present at the feast.

↑ **Third** It took three years of exhausting work to conquer this dangerous territory. Inferior people couldn't have done it — so don't give in to their demands for reward.

↑ **Second** If a loss or setback occurs, do not pursue the thief or your property. Delay the feast — for what is lost will be brought back to you within a week.

↑ **Bottom** Don't hurry to the feast. If you do not brake hard and look cautiously ahead, your chariot will overturn and tip you into a ditch.

· 64 ·

Transition

 FIRE over WATER suggests: A fox in mid-leap over a torrent.

BASIC MEANING

The little fox has got his tail wet crossing the ice and is not yet over the stream. Greater caution was needed. No progress now – but order and success will come out of this disorganized time.

MOVING LINES

Sixth Those who successfully cross a great river may, of course, celebrate. But if they overdo the wine, their success will be tarnished. To trip drunkenly and fall in the shallows would lose all respect.

↑ **Fifth** Go confidently forward: confidence breeds confidence and will bring good fortune. When you have it, don't neglect to share it generously.

↑ **Fourth** Don't give up now: this *is* the right course. Hardship and fierce activity may last for three years but dangerous territory will be subdued and you will win land and happiness.

↑ **Third** To attack now would bring disaster for you are still only half-way across the river. Go on: complete this vitally important crossing. When you are over, *then* you can act.

↑ **Second** Keep on this path: it leads to good fortune. But don't go too fast: brake your chariot now.

↑ **Bottom** He set off too hastily and fell in the stream: a set-back and humiliation.

APPENDIX

The 64 Situations of Life

If you ever find the full text of *The Little Book* obscure in relation to your question, you may consult this simplified version for assistance.

1. Persevere; this CREATIVE venture will eventually prove highly successful.
2. If you are supportive and do not attempt to take the lead, this will prove a FERTILE field.
3. Don't be deterred by a DIFFICULT BEGINNING: you are on the right track but need more help and a firmer foundation.
4. Ask advice. Give advice. Then INEXPERIENCE will be no barrier to success.
5. Be patient and WAIT. Don't act too soon.
6. Calm down and compromise. Do not persist in this CONFLICT or serious trouble will come of it.
7. You need more DISCIPLINE if this is to succeed.
8. Safety and good fortune can only be found through ACTING TOGETHER with others: therefore join or form an alliance now.
9. Be calm and patient: a long wait or IRKSOME RESTRICTIONS lie ahead.
10. This is very risky. TREADING CAREFULLY, you may succeed.
11. The difficult times are ending and HARMONY, progress and prosperity lie ahead.
12. Try to be steadfast. The good times are ending and a period of STAGNATION is coming.
13. A new ALLIANCE will bring delight if you are always open, honest and honourable.
14. You are already blessed with GREAT POSSESSIONS: they bring you further success and prosperity.
15. This can only come to a satisfactory conclusion if you act with MODESTY and moderation.
16. This plan can succeed only if you have real ENTHUSIASM for it. Have you?

17. FOLLOWING is currently more favoured than leading. Therefore let yourself be led — even by your followers.
18. Act boldly to REPAIR THE DAMAGE, making a journey if need be. Take the greatest care to ensure that what went wrong before doesn't happen again.
19. PREPARATION is necessary and you are approaching it correctly.
20. This is JUST LOOKING: it is most unlikely that anything will come of it, so don't rush or make undignified offers.
21. Be severe. A HARD BITE is necessary.
22. Concern yourself with the heart of the matter, not with ORNAMENTAL DETAILS.
23. This is a time of collapse and DISINTEGRATION. It is most unsafe to make a move of any kind.
24. Everything favours TURNING BACK to make a fresh start.
25. REMAIN entirely BLAMELESS and you will succeed. If you are in any way dishonest or dishonourable, you will fail.
26. You will succeed in the end if you spend sufficient time now BUILDING UP STRENGTH and planning ahead.
27. Provide NOURISHMENT for others first — but don't neglect your own inner needs.
28. You are not strong enough to support this DANGEROUS BURDEN — yet if you cautiously strengthen your position, prosperity and success can still be gained.
29. DANGER! You must keep very cool if you are to survive.
30. Consistently support those who depend on you for WARMTH — and gratefully welcome their help to you.
31. The ATTRACTION is great — but you should not seduce, nor be seduced. If you put a loved one's needs before your own, this can be a lasting relationship.
32. LOYALTY is favoured: you should loyally maintain the present situation.
33. A carefully controlled RETREAT now will lead to success in the end.
34. You should continue this entirely JUSTIFIED ACTION.
35. People will honour you and listen to your requests — but you will end up still SEEKING REWARD.
36. Don't let this DARKENING OF THE LIGHT destroy you. Dawn will come again.
37. Be loyal to the FAMILY. All advantage lies in simply doing your duty at home.
38. ISOLATION is hard to bear. Don't retreat further but do everything you can to move towards others.
39. A major OBSTACLE lies ahead. You can't get over it — so look for a safer route.
40. LIBERATION comes, if you will seize your chance.
41. Expect reduced circumstances and start to make REDUCTIONS now.
42. This is a fine time for EXPANSION — for major journeys and moves.

43. REFORMING ACTION is needful but dangerous. Be resolute — but cautious.
44. You are BEING CARRIED AWAY. You should not commit yourself to this venture, nor waste time dreaming about it.
45. MINGLING with friends and family will greatly help you.
46. STRIVING UPWARDS is laudable: you will succeed if you persevere and seek wise advice.
47. If you remain blameless and unbowed, you can still turn this time of EXHAUSTION and adversity into success.
48. Unless you are perfectly fit and equipped, you will be frustrated and find only THIRST AT THE WELL.
49. It's up to you. If you persevere the REVOLUTIONARY CHANGE will happen.
50. Things are out of control. However great the EMOTIONAL UPSET, a sacrifice must be made, to put things right.
51. Don't weaken or waver. If you can keep calm, success will come out of this TURBULENCE.
52. STILLNESS: the situation is unlikely to change — it is best to make no move at all.
53. If you work hard at this relationship, you will find it GROWING SLOWLY to happiness.
54. There is really nothing favourable in this PLAN. Any action you take will merely bring unhappiness.
55. Amazing and significant events are upon you: use this ABUNDANCE to the full.
56. You are merely WANDERING: this is not your real quest nor this inn your real home.
57. Greater DEDICATION is needed. Be more confident, for the winds are favourable.
58. Be truthful — and accept the TRUTH with joy, even when it is uncomfortable. Truth, by its nature, is always good.
59. Be selfless — do not cling: if a group shows signs of DISPERSING, let it do so.
60. Accept that you are REACHING THE LIMIT: you can do no more and it is unwise to try.
61. You have made the right choice. With such SERENITY WITHIN, further decisions will lead to success.
62. The times are dangerous and SAFETY LIES IN SMALLNESS: seek shelter and lie low for a time.
63. Take care! The affair may seem to be over — but great diligence and firmly honourable conduct are still needed AFTER THIS APPARENT COMPLETION.
64. This is still AN UNFINISHED STORY. Despite temporary muddles, all will be well in the end . . .

A Select Bibliography

If you seek further information on the I Ching, I recommend the following three books:

I Ching by Richard Wilhelm, rendered into English by C. F. Baynes, with a foreword by C. G. Jung. Published by Princeton University Press and Routledge & Kegan Paul.
The Book of Change by John Blofeld. Published by Mandala.
The Authentic I Ching by Henry Wei. Published by Newcastle Publishing Co.

Interesting attempts to make the I Ching useable have been made by numerous authors and publishers, including:

The Pocket I Ching, a shortened version of the Wilhelm book, by W. S. Boardman.
An Illuminated I Ching by Judy Fox, Karen Hughes and John Tampion. Published by Neville Spearman of Suffolk and Princeton University Press.

As you will know from all that I have written, I believe that the vital essence of the I Ching exists in its images, and the more words of explanation one uses, the further from that essence one travels. However, I also believe that the image-clarifications of Wen and Chou cannot be dispensed with. Finding no practical version of their work in English, I found it necessary to produce one. I wish you all the delight that I have gained from it.

Index Chart

LOWER TRIGRAM	UPPER TRIGRAM							
	DRAGON	LAKE	FIRE	THUNDER	WIND/WOOD	WATER/CHASM	MOUNTAIN	EARTH
DRAGON	1	43	14	34	9	5	26	11
LAKE	10	58	38	54	61	60	41	19
FIRE	13	49	30	55	37	63	22	36
THUNDER	25	17	21	51	42	3	27	24
WIND/WOOD	44	28	50	32	57	48	18	46
WATER/CHASM	6	47	64	40	59	29	4	7
MOUNTAIN	33	31	56	62	53	39	52	15
EARTH	12	45	35	16	20	8	23	2